SALLY BE

Pets

ANIMALS COLORING BOOK FOR ADULTS

This book may not be reproduced or trasmitted in any form or by any means, electronic or mechanical, without written permission from the author.

© 2021 Sally Berry. All Rights Reserved.

Read This Before You Start!

This book contains hand-drawn and exclusive images only. Enjoy!

Creative Therapy

Coloring is an activity which is perfect to relax and avoid stress. You can fully use your creativity, **there are no rules**. You can do it clearing completely your mind, also while listening to music, watching television or just resting. There will be some of the images you will like more and some less, but the most important thing is that you **enjoy the activity!**

Tools Advices

The paper used by *Amazon* is most suitable for soft colored pencils.
If you use them, be sure to keep them sharp so you can get a better result on every detail. If you prefer to use markers, gel pens or similar, we suggest to place an extra blank paper sheet behind your page to avoid any bleed through which might happen.
You can even take your page out of the book if you want (the pages are **NOT** perforated, but you can find on *Amazon* a tool called a page perforator for under US$ 4).

Colors Choice

We prepared for you a **color test page** at the beginning of the book. Try out at this page your colors and find the better combination. We advise to test every time the colors you want to use as sometimes they can appear in a different way on paper than what you can expect.

Experience

If you come to an image you don't feel it's suitable to be colored in this moment, leave it there, you can pick it again another day! We recommend to practice every day, it helps to be more relaxing each time.

Sharing

Please **share your work**, it's nice to see how great are you.
Read more about this at the back of this book, we have surprises for you!

We hope you have fun and enjoy this book!

Color Test Page

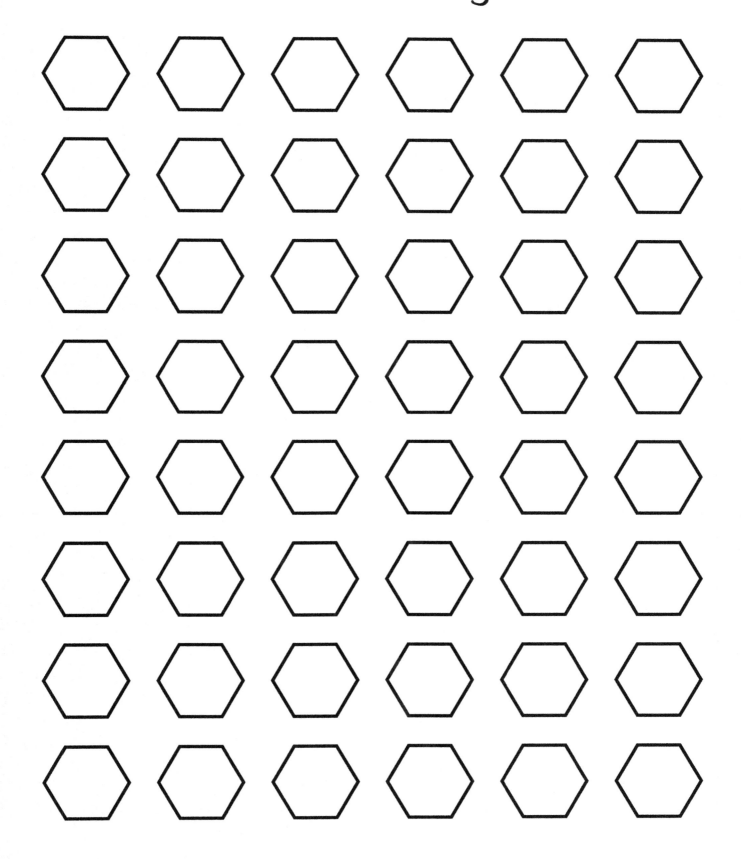

Do You Want 10 Extra Images to Download For Free?

Join our Facebook Group and Get Them Now:
https://group.sallyberrycoloring.com

We encourage to share your coloring pages done from our books on the Facebook Group, each week we run contests and you can be part of the Sally Berry Coloring Family with other enthusiast and talented coloring fans!

We need your help!

If you like this book, writing a positive review
does make a great difference for us and our future publications.

Please go on Amazon and share your experience

Review this product

Share your thoughts with other customers

Write a customer review

Find us on:

@SallyBerryColoring

@SallyBerryColoring

Sally Berry Coloring Books

COMPLETE YOUR COLLECTION OF SALLY BERRY COLORING BOOKS:

Find them all on Amazon!

Add ✓ for each book you have!

"Pets"

"Advent Calendar Vol.1"

"Advent Calendar Vol. 2"

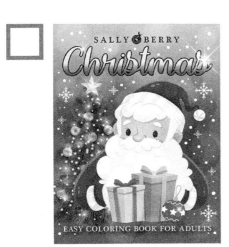
"Christmas"

"Happy Winter"

"Merry Christmas"

"Easter Holidays"

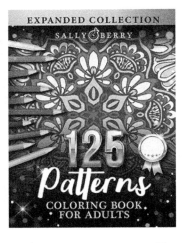
"125 Patterns"

"Halloween"

"Summertime"

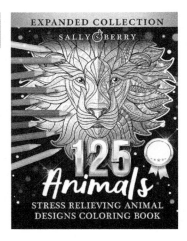
"125 Animals"

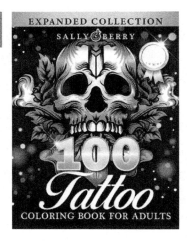
"100 Tattoo"

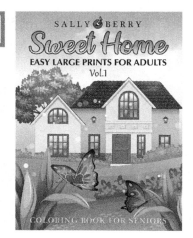
"Sweet Home" Vol.1

"Sweet Home" Vol.2

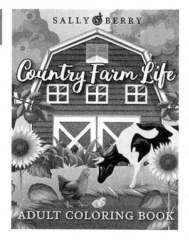
"Country Farm Life"

☐ 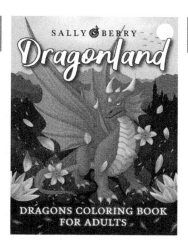 *"Dragonland"*	☐  *"Precious Animals"*	☐ 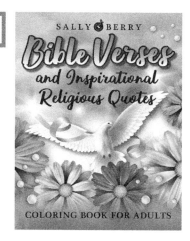 *"Bible Verses"*
☐  *"Positive Vibes"*	☐ 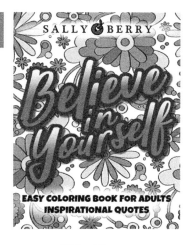 *"Believe in Yourself"*	☐ 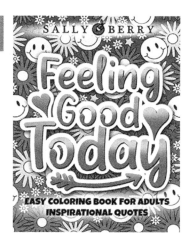 *"Feeling Good Today"*
☐  *"Flower Mandalas"*	☐  *"100 Easy Flowers"*	☐  *"Black Women"*

☐
"Witch Vibes"

☐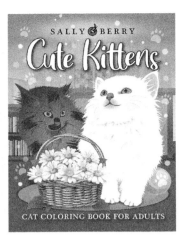
"Cute Kittens"

☐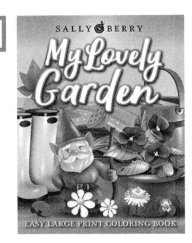
"My Lovely Garden"

☐
"Beautiful Birds"

☐
"Bloom"

☐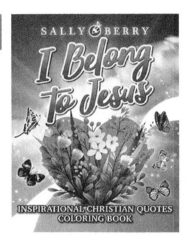
"I Belong to Jesus"

☐
"Cozy Autumn"

☐
"300 Mandalas"

Thank you for being part of the Sally Berry Family!

Printed in Great Britain
by Amazon